T0126381

sense violence • helena boberg

translated by johannes göransson

SENSE VIOLENCE

Helena Boberg

Translated by Johannes Göransson

Black Ocean
Boston - Detroit - Chicago

The cost of this translation was defrayed by a subsidy from the Swedish Arts Council, gratefully acknowledged.

Black Ocean
P.O. Box 52030
Boston, MA 02205
blackocean.org

Cover Art and Design by Janaka Stucky | janakastucky.com
Book Design by Taylor D. Waring

ISBN: 978-1-939568-31-1

Cataloging in Publication data
available at the Library of Congress

Library of Congress Control Number:

2020931990

FIRST EDITION

CONTENTS

TRANSLATOR'S NOTE

1.

The title of Helena Boberg's second book *Sinnesvåld* radiates throughout the poetry. This compound word suggests both the idea of violence against the senses and the idea that the senses enact a kind of violence. It's a book where sensuality and violence pervade every line, every sentence. I might say that it's a poem not just of ambient violence but also of violent ambience.[1] We might even say that the language is itself violent—Boberg yoking these words together into a volatile compound that cannot settle into a stable order. The violence of sense, the sense of violence.

---

1. Here I am referring to Joyelle McSweeney's phrase "ambient violence" from the article "Bringing It All Back Home" on Montevidayo.com.

2.

Boberg portrays a deeply sensual world. Everything is literally flowery:

> *The poppy has*
> *removed its red dress*
> *The throat soft and open to life*

The flowers are thickly sensual, repeatedly associated with the body and sexuality. But they are also associated with violence. With its "throat soft and open to life," the image of the poppy gives way to a line about being "opened like an egg." Like the volatile compound word of the title, the relationship between tenor and vehicle is hopelessly unstable: One minute she is addressing a literal flower with bodily metaphors, the next she is addressing a woman as if she were a flower (or an egg). The result is again a volatile ambience. As the poem notes, "words kill"— in part because they "point us out," and in part because we cannot come to "grips" with it. We are lost in its violence: "Once you have entered language you cannot get out."

3.

In this volatile atmosphere, there are suggestions of narratives — narratives that inevitably involve men who commit sexual violence against women: "You force yourself / into the girl . . . and the little / gap / bled." In this world, inner and exterior experience are mixed into a chaotic cut-up stream of consciousness where surreal hallucinations as well as social reality and samples of canonized pieces of art pass by.

The poem is concerned with the sexual violence, diminishing language, the controlling and exploiting ocular sense that surrounds and still creates the feminine subject in language, actions, and arts.

4.

Sense Violence includes a kind of baroque rewriting of the ancient Swedish folksong "Little Karin." In this tragic and morally didactic ballad, a simple peasant girl is raped and eventually tortured to death by being thrown into a "spike barrel" by the seven young servants of the king, for rejecting his courtship. Boberg's poem exposes the violence subsumed in this traditional song via a double exposure of the ballad and descriptions of contemporary events in shady discussions on Internet forums.

From the ballad (and other similar ballads), Boberg takes not just the motif of sexual violence, but also various archaic words (such as "svennar") and the allegorical-sensual, baroque logic of poetic language. The difference, perhaps, is that Karin is freed from the torture when she is transformed into a white dove whilst *Sense Violence* offers far less hope of escape. It is full of "Little Karins" kings and servants, full of acts of sexual violence.

5.

The book also samples canonical Swedish modernist poet Gunnar Ekelöf's "Mölna-Elegi." Readers need not know this specific book to sense something of that great modernist poem of the poet moving through the excitement of modern spaces (think Blaise Cendrars, think Guillame

Apollinaire). Like those predecessors, the language is feverishly intensive. In difference to them, the spaces the *I* moves through are fraught and dangerous.

6.

Readers of Swedish poetry will no doubt see in Boberg's book a lineage that includes such prominent poets as Ann Jäderlund, Aase Berg, Lars Norén, and Eva Kristina Olsson. But there is no reason to limit Boberg to some kind of national canon. She's widely read and in her extreme drama, American readers may see connections to American poets Sylvia Plath and Louise Glück or maybe more contemporary poets whose work explores the fraught zone where taste and tastelessness touch, such as Danielle Pafunda or Cathy Wagner, even if Boberg has not read them. We might also think of HD's classic imagist poem, "Garden," except the "garden" has been blown up by the heat. My mind is also brought to several baroque Latin American writers such as Alejandra Pizarnik and Marosa Di Giorgio. Poetry crosses boundaries.

7.

American discussions about translation have recently tended to foreground the choices and strategies of the translator, making out of her a kind of ersatz author. It's an honorable effort to raise the appreciation and visibility of the translator, but I think it perhaps makes us too sovereign. The truth is that I translate the way the book asks me to. And this book asks me to translate feverishly. To enter into burning and volatile atmosphere and to translate from that space.

8.

My own childhood also involved a double exposure to song and violence. As a child in '70's Sweden, I was educated through and immersed in the kinds of violent-yet-anesthetized folk songs Boberg re-animates here, while also being trained up on pastiches of American murder-ballads by listening with my mother to Bob Dylan records. Which of these was my mother tongue? Can the son's ear be a kind of orifice, where the poison of language, song, poetry pours in? My later displacement as a teenage immigrant to America further distorted my relationship to both bodies of song. Working closely with Helena to translate this poetry, I found myself again in both a displaced and familiar position, suspended amid naturalized and denaturalized relationships to Swedish and American folk songs, amid the Swedishes and Englishes that transpose themselves at every instance in my ear, amid the distance and immediacy of folk and contemporary violence. In this double experience of estrangement and familiarity the body of song conjured by Boberg became new to me, fatal and volatile. Like the medieval figure of the Gothic maiden or her bewitched knight, I found myself in thrall. I have attempted to open my throat and pass this song along to new listeners, in all its piercing and uncanny intricacy. My only method was to let the intensity pour through.

— Johannes Göransson

SENSE VIOLENCE

PREDATORY DRIVE

Still there is red behind the lobe
she sticks in a finger
The small one
it seems to laugh
Note a hard figure
against its innards

Honey eye!

Still blinks
fur glossy but warm

She hones, fades
her paw sharp
A rhythm wells up
with dry sounds

and ivory
The porous jaw
and new sounds

Quiet little tongue
remember the good food
The bell is silent
my belly cramps
the slack shadow
blind to my lament

Furiously I ride toward the center
push out the innards there

A tight string snaps its fragile fuzz-ear
The sense-violent female
and fat garb
Breaths getting sloppier
Wet-nose!
She tears at the drum
the torn entity
smudged
Wants to tease, tear

lay like a wreath and tighten

Laps in what is possible
fat paste, urine drops, linty stains
Deep hole drilled into throat, smoothglossy
made of ebony, tart
but drained in eternity
The little drink!
Come, pâté

She covers herself in down!
defiled and stained
Roaring silk flower
jealous and yellow

Her hand cupped around my neck

can crack and love

like food

Now the eye-slit is narrower, clothed

Landed flat

with palms and scent

Let the innards flow

That mouth eats from everything

and rumps down without permission

               Hungers
          for your tongue
          as for
             salted butter

We dreamed together
     about the state before childhood
when we could not yet talk

                    The gaze turned
               toward drowsy memories

          Girls
     their hair swims in the wind

Observe like an animal
of wild voices
               Trying
               again to push
               into the dream

               Every conversation
               an invasion

               The neighbor woman
               with this night's cigarette
               She looks
               straight at me

Her eyes
The withdrawn
gaze

Exposed like
a captured animal

The
too-soft hair
that will not
grow

a Botticelli angel

Alone
like
a silk stocking
in the dawn-
weeping

Touches the memory of a bird
with spread-out feathers

Rounded
like rose petals
At the root
pale red

I didn't want to destroy

l eat from
her body
so that I will
never grow

Her face
moves
in mine

: without purpose or reason

Cool my cheek
the sadness is
too great
to wear around

As a word
she no longer
exists
outside me

The men in the city
 with stiff snakes
  in their hands
 Want to make the earth clean and beautiful again
While desire flutters around them
 they search for rich hidden milk-veins
 among maimed bodies
  whose raw fumes excite them
   in ever widening circles

 Where have they learned this perdition so deep and disguised?

  The chaotic bodies
       that are still alive
  —do they hide something in their organs' inner chaos?
Children shatter their own eyes with living stones
       The women's bellies swelling
   algae sacs
    in the tracks of these forceful rites
The images gradually harden and the game
  calms down
   Elastic time
compresses these moments
 into meaningless rhymes
     Blossom again into split tongues

This is where the disenchantment of the world begins

     and the moon falters

The poppy has
removed its red dress
The throat soft and open to life

Away from this place

Let me

be opened

like an egg

Your face
appeared in my memory

Why
does it remind me
of nothing

Beloved
velvet chin
nut eye
child
To me you remain drowned

Day rests in its garbage bag

All that remains
the silence that has taken possession of me
:that is to say clichés
in their simplest forms

The cigarette-breast at night
and youth flees
like a swallow
Girls' hair float
in space
                              The eternal drowsiness
                                          I am
                                     in plural
                              small drowsies
                                      that run
                                     catch up
                                        exhale
                         in one and the same cloud
The light, round
movement
and the day
goes out
                                 Drowning-
                                   sleep

Everything begins
and ends
at exactly
the right time
and place

Say it
that my breath
is milk
and the girl
loosens
without her mother
while the nails
grow and are clipped
and cigarettes
run out

What comes after joy

The trigger and the crosshairs
Mother without child

I tail after
and beg for mother (Nothing happens
until everything is over)

The tongues of bells
in the break between
death and life

The flow of saliva
that pours out and back

The snake's twisted body
a braid of closely related lusts

Green-shimmering
forms
that enclose
coming nearer
And the vice is summer's innocent infant

O
red sister
I follow
your tracks closely
as if
you dragged me along
in your collapse
   Torn as you

          C a l m

                An embryo
                that lets go

                Hovering landscape
                my middle
                and Saturn ring

                Stiff
                is the thought
             interrupted

Turn around your mouth!

Where flesh still lingers

Mine bleeds
Rose-fingered
White-armed
Pearl-eyed
Black like ebony

Bones scraped
—She must have scratched herself on thorn-bushes

Her hands badly hurt
nails missing
or are torn apart

The little one with
cracked body
The asphalt's
wart
to cut into
Only a cunt

How funny they look from here . . .
all these people who exist
without purpose or meaning . . .
Like ants on the ground

The skin blossoms
jasmine on the chest
or lilies, lis—
Glass iris
Fullmoonsick
You force yourself
into the girl

I hurt

The intestine burst
and the little
gap
bled
The Lords jabbed
with pink snakes
in the silk bed

The bell is larger
than me am

The bell is more large
than me am

The clock-face stunted
goldsheen
fleeing braid

Like a sonar
the child screams
or we do
Let it happen
beneath the moon

Look out for the poisonous snakes

Push it in
so that the jaw
slackens
and the pelvis
drops

Play with the thought
animals sniff
everything

Blast off

The boys love
each other
smooth fingers
transparent geniuses

On the third day
the membrane drops
Bloodblack

The loveliest sweetness

Then they tear
it out
with a probe
Petals of blood
blossom
in formaldehyde

Oh peonies
never has beauty
been so violent

I wash myself in other bodies

The dark summer
closes its eyes

Drools its water

against clinking ground
Water pearls
                    That man
                    is so beautiful

The flowers hunger
as for breast milk

Latesummernothingatall
sails
parallel to the sun's cranium
The neck almost
comes loose

            The throat soft and open to life
Lily-red cleft-lip
            The heavy flour-breast
that powders

I want to return to everything
rain simple things hatred
opened up to the marvelous

Dream about the sanitarium
its set boundaries
        White cube
        where we moved
        freely
acted
    insane

                    :Girlwomen, Warty Cabbage, She-foxes
                                        Sneaking
                                along the corridors
                                            walls
                                all hours of the day
                                    Signs in the air
                        constantly laugh-whispering
                                        Living lips
                                    without words
                                        Begging
                                    for sweets
                                    cigarettes
                                    electroshocks
                                        a lay
                                    Anything
                                    to numb
                    Crooked high heels torn wrists
                            Menstruation-red lips
                        Murderous, dragging, hissing
                                        hatred

*"There once was
a bird. Good lord."*

I live with the image of you as an infant

Your eyes are so lonely

I am sure that you are more beautiful than the birds over there

> *The world eats, will always eat*
> *Nothing is as contagious as evil*

"Any place could be sad. Tough, if it's in you"

> *It is the eye that is dark*

Sometimes I have awoken at night
I don't know how

I have given birth to your child
It makes me sick

You probably understand that

> *Do I know where it comes from*

Depression like a raw throat
This which is also a language

You are newborn
sunk into chlorine

On the upper lip pearls
Just beyond

I love your skull

You seem to be drugged
and maybe you are

If I fumble for you
I don't know if you exist
Now you flow, permeable
Thickets keep you from reaching

I own you as if you were my own child

You tempt me toward the dark bath
where I will cease

I accept everything you do
not out of love
but out of a sheer hunger for power

Now we journey
toward the source
or the chasm
Without any resistance
I nurse both of us

In the egg-sack's pink membrane
a cut
  :Out trickles the universe

The hissing snake
and the summer
that is no longer
mine

Weak voices
that do not cohere
Thinking becomes brief

The mold flowers
fully bloomed
coronary artery

                              Or the child
                              inexhaustible
                              drills into
                              the world

    Without memory's consent
      :the peach's fuzzy cheek
      the finger straight in hard
        the sweet flesh
          taste of iron
          breast sugar
      The snake spills—

The large pit
against the palate
hard and slippery and sour

The grape juice coarse
in the fuzz
and the stiff dream

The moment well chosen

The slumber
and the lost time
(If I lose it
it has never existed—
only the
decomposed body
and the secret lives of insects)

:Hover in the wonderful, honeyed light
let the dreams wash through the skin
The sounds from the street, people's
movements
take place in me

The shadow of a strange man moves through the room

His soft scent

Day without images
The sounds fill a blind existence
The I is only an event

Electric
Overexposed urge

The red staring flowers
with frilly filaments
Dizzying hair

                    The boys spill
                      enormous
                        drops
                        of glass

            The stiff face
            of a clock
            The deaf snake
            and the summer that was taken from me

        The decomposition process
        and what follows
        The dark demand
:a weird greeting from the other side

                  I step inside the man

Your sunroom
the rumbling bells
and the mist-veiled mountains

Lose ourselves us on the ledge
just at mid o'clock

All memories candied
trembling ant eggs

a show of intimacy
—one lacks all defenses

Grab for invisible objects
Make oneself tight
for a feverish milk

Leftovers that don't belong
appear
in sleep
Twisted into screams

You observe
with eyes
like mine shafts

Transform me
to a rage

I act
until you can't
take anymore

Steal from silence
until I own it
Then speak
Speak similarly

The sound of the kitchen fan
like a state of mind

Yet another woman
in the window

Hair like rubies
She washes dishes
lit from beneath

The heavy curtain

I think she is happy

Unreal beings
move
on the other side of the street

The man on the balcony
observes
:Hair like rubies
silk skin
Pure and utter cabaret

Twilight growing cramped. Makes itself more cramped

The hand spreads an innocent content

                                        Night's flower
                                     devours the words
                                      loose as oysters
                    Shows me
                    its flaking pistil

The Girls
　　　　their hair swim in the breeze
　　　　Lifts
And the speech
　　　　selfmirroring
　　　　They dream
　　　　with words
　　Become
　　glide away
　　like saliva

　　The Lords dance
　　　　with red golden bands

　　　　　　Dance and close their eyes so near

and the full moon glows as if it were made of glass

　　　　　　　　The girls dream wild games

　　　　　Tempt out
　　　　　　the raw and the blind

　　　Soft lining
　　　invites
　　　to party

The Men in the city
get joy
to make up for all their sorrows

        The wind cools, the sun burns

The Girl follows wherever they want
    Oh the king's young men
    they roll her around and around

        (How lovely to share like brothers)

They number seven
    as noblemen disguised

        The rooster crows, sit safely in the saddle!

    Seven times flayed
    she smiled and disappeared

Then we sit down
contemplate

        :Was she cunning enough?

    All of us possess a certain power to love tear apart

but the eye demands its fill of rose and lipstick clean-shaven peaches lords
    carry boots her mouth is a tulip

She is so naked and unique

The still warm smell
of a mass of people
remains
in her body
which is ours
or who

(How irritating that the images disappear
  and still: in their aggressive absence take over
One drop
at the hem of the skirt
says
they really did exist once)

I search for the gaze I have been denied

Mulberries
heavy
in the tree
Drown
everything
in
swollen honey
The black garters
alone on the cliff
the marzipan of the Valentine Cake
attracts more and more ants
Earwigs look through
every nook and cranny
"She had fled, she was dead"

So naked and unique

Lord of the seed
lord of the sheep

You are the mask I try to construct
Wanting to give birth to a new order

Hair that flutters like smoke
and eyes like a blinking doll

A furious flower
follows

                                          the scripted ritual
                                          that precedes
                                          every act of violence

                        Let her fall
                        like a life
                        or night

        Your child will be mine
           I will speak through its mouth

                    She hangs like a ripe fruit from the tree
                    Still dripping

                        We see straight into the center of violence
                        Your dreams flow out between the trees
                            and I was crazy from forgetting

                                        :a stiff hole

        Cheek veined
        like that of a just-awakened infant

                    Nourishment pulses through us

                            Tear the dream with me
                            at birth
                            into this

It is a mixture of animals, herbs, wedding couples without faces

The soft room

                                        Who will
                                  again birth me
                                          dead

It is like the story where nothing ends and nothing begins

And I wanted to reach you but you were me
and the water was so dark

                                  Now light

                              She versifies sanguinely
                        pushes her verbiage into my mouth

I eat everything she has ever played
              (See myself as a swan that dips its head in the mirror)

                        :mortal perfection
                        between two forgotten dreams

              (Something will split us apart. I don't yet know what)

The castrated animal
its hyperventilating gaze
begs
for mercy

Unpredictable
with its wounds

Or I have been chosen
as victim

                                        I drown
                                        in the day
                                        with a
                                        slowly
                                        rolling wave
                                        in my head
                                        The mundane
                                        :a gap

An undecided transparent
gray atmosphere
        the concepts cannot reach

    Then I returned
Gaze mute
    from all the impressions without meaning

                        I won't be here much longer

                                High summer rain
                                    and blue
                                eyes, one of which
                                    has darkened

            Charred
            Served
            as an oyster
            between lust
            and madness

Small warm bodies
fall off
like pinecones
or eggs

                                        Topple
                              through a window
                              let yourself hatch

                Not yet ready to fall

            The entire tree crown
            contorts
            from vertigo

                              loses its fruit
                              at the mere touch

    Lose yourself
    I say

                              Everything begins
                              and ends
                              at exactly
                              the right time
                              and place

The sensitivity
How he holds me
                    Hypnotic fragrance

(What comes after joy)

                    Possessed
                                        Possessed until paralyzed
                    Appear as a s y m p t o m
Forgetful from language

                    Return
Hall with ruined women
They stand in a ring and laugh

                                        hysterically

        I am dancing in the middle
            like a naked animal

                            The waltz with uncertain outcome
                    Beg for refuge
            Apart
                    tongue

                                        Universe in cross section
                    The substance that remains

                                        marriage
                                                    and animals
            I am a lady

                                        The chasm
                    between geniality and superiority

                                A stone that laughs in the sun

    Speech open in all directions not knowing where it comes from
            or where it is heading

                            Time brings many promises in its bosom
                            :freedom wifedom fruitfuldom

                                            A dance is brewing
                            Plump bosoms we are so thankful for

    A well-adjusted clockwork (in the Lord's time)
                            Oh we whirl around

                    Beyond the dance
                            stiff images
            My sight blocked
            by staring animals

The body awakes in darkness

Silence is not the absence of something
Everything shouts against everything

An insect tries to flee
out of the room
Flutters, bumping desperately
(Neither moist heat nor the moon affects its yearning)

Nerves and dance
Around the sun's smooth plate a ring of light blood
The bodies' dragonflylife

Words kill when they label us
(The more one tries to grip them, the more one is gripped by them)
Mute about these sudden disappearances

There's a threat in the light

Pale spring with marbled nights
Places where one loses one's bonds and bearings

People wracked
watermelons on asphalt

A lonely woman who lives
like 1 unblossomed flower
    The forest and ocean hurt, mimic it

                The man spills
            poison and hunger

      It is so dark and beautiful
        A lonely egg loosens

    I seduce you into my chasm *the cliff where roses blossom*
        Long for your breath

    The invisible arms that carry

Sought a state of mind in which it would finally be possible to merge
with the substances and poisons to which we are exposed: The sign's
uncleanliness a small glowing jewelry *like a crocus, still enclosed in
its own body*

Once you have entered language you cannot get out

The taut apricot
paints her mouth wet

       A jab opens death
          this summer already
              where the fruit violates its sisters

Count your amusements
:1 split fig (rotting)
Blonde dreams
as light as the soul of a corpse
Limbs camouflaged with fruit
(It is natural that women should be picked in that season
& they are always smaller than they should be)

The neighbor woman sleeps
Thoughtfully she observes death
as an object between gratification and pain
She has grown pale and yet
she is full of longing   Prey for the boys' arrogance
Smiles at despair
The cigarette still glows
The dream
a room
inside
the body
with the enclosed appearance of an object

Lower your voice when you speak about summer
When tasting a fruit it's the palate that matters

For the soul is fooled
unaware that girls languish
in the meadow

:Mothers like dewdrops
maidens like dewdrops
mole-darkness inside
My mother who found it so difficult to smile at the days' passing

                                        (I myself anxious
                                        barely human at all
                                        in that way I want
                                        without ever having had
                                        a desire
                                        for anything but sleep
                                        The thought is limp like milky
                                        high-summer oysters

:Foams through days: the latesummerdarkness
barely viable
Twilight every hour of the day: depth perception eliminated
The world two dimensional

Humans maybe three-dimensional shadows
The laughs take place outside of me

                                        —In some ways
                                        I am a clinic
                                        with room for one)

I will die like an exposed bell in this vast desolate hall?

The arrogance of males reaps triumphs:

A genius is born!
Come, celebrate celebrate
So sophisticated and unique
His name is dead no sweet
We recognized his great spirit
(how objective)

Possessed, humbled
want to submit
(do the words belong to nobody in particular?)
with whitening lips like violets

She flees
with loosened hair
a gash in her back

(how feminine)
She bows to
the will of the masters
Like a fragile bluebell
Her folded
petals
in shreds
and her eye is clouded

She eats of it
until
she overflows

(I don't want anybody to see how much of this I have devoured
Every morning day night one has to one's existence meaningful
You who have always loved womankind: was it I who sewed
these pieces from rags?)

This continues at a regular pace
like the rhythm of plants
Like through long and deep breathing
every male-stalk
swells up
lowers itself on the crown
and spills
its sap

Excretes it

and then catches its breath
for further
amusements

Innocent prey whose flesh has ripened in the sun
and the moon hides the pedophilia of beasts

These bloodless lips
that tighten
from tension
and assume
the color of violets
(A color I truly appreciate)
At the same time her
round wide-
open mouth
toward which
the whole room
bends

The birds that slept inside my head
I do not want to know more than I find out when I touch her
Where are your eyes my girl?

Today
I recognize
a hungry
human
Not from the voice
but the eyes
that deflower
instead of observing

He moves
with the finger
across
the fruit peel
Wriggles along the notch
until the flesh grows juicy
and already
the world's fragrance
rises from the ground

(This is not the kind of man who makes women happy)

And the peach paints the little mouth
—She is a figurine, expensive, made of Chinese porcelain—
Where does she come from
she who has wandered astray
on our
sidewalks

Then the men gather
(because of her
dress)
in clusters
Call on her
with their
shuddering snakes
How funny they look from here

:Same kinds of hands
on the same kinds of
breasts
And the egg
runs
from her
mouth

The fertile
darkness's
raw fumes
fool
the mouth
into begging
like a sick person
for
the electroshocks'
releasing spasm
the muffled cigarette smoke
or the sweets
that fix
one's own palate
in the middle of the world
Rage
a foreboding
side effect

Isn't it true that
tongues have
never collapsed
as in
the hall
for ruined
bitches
lords
geniuses
Our games
resembled
ballets
of poorly
maneuvered
marionettes
An inverted social order
with a narcotic aftertaste
where balance is reached
in a sleeping
state
Rage
a foreboding
side effect

We slept and slept

Promiscuous fallen fruit
with a pain
that fell asleep with us
But started over as soon as we again
opened our eyes

In the same moment
as the temporal bones
were anaesthetized
for the electricity's
symmetrical branching-out
which would fill me
with a
fantastic happiness
I was taken
to this sorrow chasm
of all things' inner time

(It's long ago,
the shout was another)

There is only this violent
human society
which resembles a sullen mind

Come o come amaryllis
The heart is a tedious animal
Seeks the marvelous
in the mundane

Downpour of clouds
into the leaf-tree's light-
shifting red
mouths

Is summer finally over

A fever globe up high
blinding and inflamed

Hard-shining
through
the cloud-
bed
where I lay
with my gruel-
belly
baby thighs
mommy-sick

all the way
into the honey-
cup's
raw
mouththroat

But lovelier
to me
than the night's
cruel
raging games
with dripping candles

dipped
in dark-violet
velvet bells
that
have been opened up
with a knife

Yes, that's where you stick it in

Smaller
and larger
nooks
of still living cell-
tissue

The irradiated
manna
which later
wakes her face
Yellow
beneath the
pregnant
moon
They have
helped themselves
Scarfed down
Eaten
of her lipstick
and
her daughters
(Lovely little decorations)

And I
:lost in the city
like 1 slutty satin flower
but unaware of it
With nagging mouth-
sores below

(The only thing I'm thinking is that I want out of my own body)

I fled night and day but I never got away

                                    —Lovelier
                                    for me
                                    would be
                                    to return
                                    to the sleep-
                                    shell's
                                    deaf windings
                                          where the feeble dreams
                                          hold existence in balance

To get to float away in a breathtaking, blackening, unspeakable dream

    Evening was falling and I felt his eyes but did not know who he was
How strong was the fragrance of carnations that came to me in the dream
          It rose
                  as steam
          from skin
          and giblets
In the moonlight my hands become strangely white and useless
                              and my chaotic shouts
                                      resemble mute wax casts

The moon sews your face to the darkness
                              Open the mouth and receive
The dream that grows in the sleeper's life
:a multicolored eye that cannot see anything

                    (it is there even if I cannot talk about it)

On the bottom of a dark summer
A city as soft as a body
Reminiscent of a cut-through brain
The women move
like beautiful shiny
animals
in the violet twilight
A wakeful eye follows
every step they take

Grown men with strangely stiff bodies
pitter-patter like cats around a plate of porridge (want to get in the manger)
Say that
the only truth
is love beyond all reason
& Lovely is the lusty
seductive game of desire
& Death is the most ingenious of us all   (Hurrah)
Their mold-dreams resemble naked animals
Ready to mate
:Why were the roses most yellow in the east, the lilies whitest in the west;
in the south the rumps were the fattest; in the north the dieted busts
were pale and teensy-weensy small

Inside the storm the storm is a cloud that stands still
As if a latesummer wind brushed in under the dress
a male cuckoo egg & a dance of roses

Yet another time I touch
the hungry
fold
  This time
  in sleep
A sloppy faded-
  out
bit of silk
  filled with darkness
    out of which
        a jerky
      surging
    incoherent
      speech
    streams
A
sleep-
  less
inner
  child

                                        These
                                          de-
                                        composed
                                        plant parts
                                          that
                                          like
                                          in-
                                        testiness
                                        corrode
                                        the air

Solve
soon
dis-
solved

—Where are you heading, mortal
striking desperately against the walls

Blood is the true color of humans

Wide awake inside sleep
with a surging wave beneath the skin

Resting day
bewilderingly
    similar

            Outside
        they talk
        about the winter
        that is
        coming
            or
        is it already
        here
:Stuffs
the loneliness
        And the dream
                turns around
                invades
                with new strength
                As in a hospital ward

—That is "society"

My electricity is weak

This
is
a love-
story
with
a happy ending
or without

(I am dripping of love or thirst)

& The lily-white women problems
appear in a new light
when everything is for sale

I have no sense of humor
or feeling of human superiority

Cleave
the crown of creation
That is to say brings me along (or mourns)
:Sticking my own body into the soft flesh mass
assuming a shared body temperature
The homeless have enclosed themselves in cocoons of blankets
torn cardboard boxes

Summer returns to the city's intestines
  with tasty sweetness
Like lords and bees do

  Mouths blossom like flowers
  :A joy sharp as basil

      And the flowers are actually murderous
      Bells that drone and roar

I am dying
of thirst
for nourishment

  While the lunatics sleep like inlaid pearls
that have been pried out of their black-blue shells
for a more orderly life
  of straight lines

    Poisoned into obscurity

        (We decline exotic fruit
        and erotic debauchery
        aside from the ordinary pattern
      of the home-pudenda resp. the forced mating
  which accd. to calculations will take place, based purely on statistics)

Sprawl communities shoot up like sprouts
as a result of reasonable seeds
Ants bite into the poisoned ground
Males are so dependent on the myth
(They deserve medals for that)

—they demand no more than to obey and admire

In every nook behind every window
in the breathtaking bodies of the bluecementhouses
small dish-washing, whispering
existences, bent over frying pans, nursing babies
and shopping lists
Family providers
parasites
who however
draw their straws
but prefer to play video games
full-time (we know that)

& when the same summer dream
as Lords (who at the same time are capable of producing such societal
benefits as arms manufacturers, fake and real tans and equity stocks

—Yes they are a delight for soul and eye)

(The man is a burden on society & a woman is a utopia & at the top of the food-
chain are those who work on other things)

The vapid afternoon
: a vacuum that protectively closes itself off

Each and every one dances in their own
dazed
loneliness
Choked by intoxication

The body's lovely weight ceases
where the night and the moss are smooth
Swell up against the melee of everything
The scent becomes a part of my pulse

Bluefrozen like a shell in November
I eat from the source of my mystical life-cycle

(my ruined souvenir)

& make love in this way to life
Become pregnant with ovaries hissing of violent love

ABOUT THE AUTHOR

Helena Boberg (b. 1974) works as a poet, translator and editor. Her books include *Repuls* and *Sinnesvåld.* She's got a background in the surrealist movement and she is part of the international network Shaerat, female poets in Sweden and the Middle East.

ABOUT THE TRANSLATOR

Johannes Göransson (b. 1973) is the author of six books of poetry including *The Sugar Book, Transgressive Cirulation: Essays on Translation* and the forthcoming memoir *POETRY AGAINST ALL.* He is also the translator of books by Aase Berg, Ann Jäderlund, Johan Jönson, Henry Parland, and Kim Yideum. He teaches at the University of Notre Dame and edits Action Books.